THE ULTIMATE REMOTE JOBS GUIDEBOOK

Make Money From The Comfort of Your Home!

Judy S. Berman

Table of Contents

INTRODUCTION

Welcome to " THE ULTIMATE REMOTE JOBS GUIDEBOOK " In today's digital age, the traditional 9-to-5 office job is no longer the only path to a successful career. With the rapid advancement of technology and the internet, a whole new world of opportunities has opened up, allowing individuals to work from the comfort of their own homes. Whether you're looking for more flexibility, seeking to escape the daily commute, or aiming to achieve a better work-life balance, this book is your comprehensive guide to navigating the exciting realm of online jobs. We'll explore various remote work options, provide valuable tips on how to excel in this virtual environment, and help you unlock the full potential of a fulfilling and prosperous work-from-home career. Let's embark on this journey together and transform the way you work.

Chapter 1: Use Instagram Marketing

Instagram has grown significantly in the realm of social media in recent years.

With more than 500 million active users each month, Instagram has emerged as a preferred social media platform for many businesses.

These companies are currently investing a sizable portion of their social media budget in Instagram to increase their customer and lead generation.

Therefore, now is the ideal time to profit from Instagram's rising popularity.

If you are willing to put in the time and work, you may expand your Instagram account to a point where it can earn you a significant amount of money online.

Appropriate For :

- Those who enjoy taking pictures and using Instagram.

Skills Necessary :

- Ability to take high-quality photos.

- Professional photo editing skills.

- The ability to use apps like Canva, Befunky, etc. to alter high-quality photographs or backgrounds.

- Imagination and creativity.

Starting Points

All you need to get started is an Instagram account, a charming username, a lovely profile photo, and an intriguing bio.

You are prepared to post and launch your marketing campaign if you have these elements in place.

Tips

Choose your specialty

Before you can begin marketing on Instagram, you must decide on a market niche.
The easiest method to identify a specialty that is right for you is to think about the areas that you are most passionate about or skilled at.

For instance, if you love fashion and like to keep up with the current trends, you can open an Instagram account and routinely share styles, tips, and tricks with your followers.

Correctly complete your bio

Your bio is the first place potential followers may learn about you.
Therefore, you must ensure that it leaves them with the best possible first impression. You can use emoticons, a one- or two-line explanation, and links to your website to draw attention.
To make sure the correct kind of followers can find you easily, you can also include a few keywords and a few hashtags.

Write content for your ideal audience

Before you begin publishing photographs to your account, conduct some research to see what your target audience is most interested in.

Which pictures will they find appealing? Which taglines will resonate with them the most? so forth.

Finding the answers to the aforementioned questions will enable you to make targeted posts that will attract a large number of loyal followers to your account.

Post frequently

You should publish numerous photographs each day if you want to increase your following quickly.

However, be careful not to post them all at once; space them out over the day.

When you're too busy to post multiple pictures, strive to at least post one per day.

Utilize just photographs of the highest caliber

Your Instagram account needs to be a brand. Therefore, be sure to publish only the best-looking, high-quality photographs.

Posting photographs of poor quality serves no use because they all lower the worth of your account.

High-quality photographs not only help to catch the attention of the many casual browsers who will only discover you because your high-quality image caught their attention, but they also help to create a lasting visual impression in the minds of your followers, thereby growing your following.

Utilize relevant hashtags

Hashtags are Instagram's most important feature, and if you utilize them strategically, they can help your posts get in front of millions of users who could be interested in your profile.

Make sure you include the finest hashtags for your niche in every post by doing some research and finding them.

To get the most popular tags in your niche, go to the website **Tagsforlikes.com.**

Additionally, try not to overuse hashtags and keep them relevant. You can use up to 30 hashtags per post on Instagram.

Interact with your followers

You need to interact with your followers to establish trust and gain an understanding of their issues, needs, and expectations so that you can use pbl information to provide them with more pertinent content.

By liking their photos, leaving insightful comments, or even following them back, you can easily interact with the followers you already have or those you hope to gain within your niche.

Even better, you can hold regular competitions that your followers might find interesting.

For instance, a well-known watch company runs a "Pic of the Day" competition in which they ask their customers to submit pictures of themselves wearing the brand's watches.

They then decide which of the submitted images they like the best, and they upload it to their Instagram account.

Such competitions are popular with followers because, if chosen, they can gain recognition among the brand's other fans.

How to Make Money

The best ways to monetize Instagram are as follows:

Affiliate marketing

This is a good way to start earning money, especially if your Instagram following is rapidly increasing and your account has a few thousand followers.

Instagram affiliate marketing is very different from other conventional platforms like blogging and video marketing.

Here, you must upload eye-catching pictures of the goods you want to promote to increase sales. You should also include your affiliate URL in your bio or caption.

The URLs of a select few well-known businesses where you can register as an affiliate and get started are as follows:

- Shareasale.com

- Stylinity.com

- Liketoknow.it

Produce sponsored articles

You can make good money by writing sponsored posts for brands if your followers are highly engaged.

A sponsored post is simply a regular post with a high-quality image or video showcasing a brand or product.

For each sponsored post, you are compensated. Payment varies according to your following's popularity, influence, engagement, and other factors.

Any sponsored post should have the goal of increasing brand or product awareness among your followers.

But while doing so, be careful to only pick brands or products that are appropriate for your audience and complement your Instagram personal brand.

The companies listed below, along with their names and websites, allow you to sign up as an influencer:

Tapinfluence 1

1.Following exact URL: https://influencers.tapinfluence.com/sign_ up

2.Influenz

(Exact website address: https://www.ifluenz.com)

Takumi

3.(Exact URL- https://takumi.com./app)

selling your pictures

Why not sell the high-quality photos you take and expertly edit them for your Instagram posts to earn some extra money?

Numerous people, bloggers, and companies are always looking for fresh and imaginative images.

You can find them and sell your photos using Instagram.

There is a very easy way to accomplish this. Your images should have a watermark, and the caption should include a complete list of all the selling and contact information.

You can sell your shots to people who contact you and express interest in buying them.

The names of a few reliable websites where you can sell your Instagram photos are listed below.

- Twenty20.com

- Foap.com

Market your goods

If you are a retailer or a product creator, you should use Instagram to its full potential to increase sales.

Instagram is a great platform for product promotion because you can post unique, personalized photos of your products that aren't available anywhere else.

You can employ a variety of marketing strategies, such as designing eye-catching infographics, asking current clients to post pictures of themselves using your product, or even posting images of the actual raw materials and production process.

Market your Instagram profile

If you have amassed millions of followers on Instagram and have already achieved fame.

Your goals have all been met, or you simply need to stop using Instagram and start doing something else.

You'll be glad to know that you can sell your Instagram account and make a sizable sum of money if you decide to stop using Instagram.

Your Instagram account's cost will vary depending on its niche, follower count, engagement rate, and other factors.

A few trustworthy websites where you can sell your Instagram account are listed below:

- Fameswap.com

- Viralaccounts.com

- Extra Advice

The best ways to monetize your Instagram account are those that have been mentioned above once you have a few thousand followers, but I advise you to hold off on starting any promotions until you have 10,000 followers.

Some of you might think it's crazy to wait until an account has 10,000 followers before beginning to make any money.

But trust me, it's the right approach.

Your followers must first develop a positive opinion of you in their minds, and the only way to do that is by consistently giving them value over time.

Chapter 2: Do Pinterest Marketing

Look at today's social media world scenario; you'll see Facebook and Twitter are ruling it. Large companies and online businesses spend tons of money on advertising on these platforms. It helps them to acquire more customers and grow their businesses, but they are so focused on using the platforms mentioned above that they completely ignore one powerful platform, and that is Pinterest. Now let me explain how you can leverage this situation for making more online. But first, look at its facts below.

Pinterest has over 100 million active users and 176 million registered users, out of which 71% are women.

It's good news if you are trying to sell a product that is relevant to women customers. You can showcase your products to a mostly female audience with very less effort

93% of its users have bought something online.

This is a great sign as most of its users are accustomed to online shopping. That means they are confident about making online purchases and you don't need to convince them or mainly gain their trust to sell your online products

Pinterest has two important features

- First, it allows visitors to enjoy its Pins without signing up

- Second, Pinterest boards rank high in search engines

Both the features mentioned above allow you to leverage Pinterest's authority in search engines and help you reach audiences that are not even on Pinterest, thus hugely amplifying your reach at no cost. For example, take a look at the following image: In this image, you can see that I searched the keyword "birthday party ideas," you can also see on the red box that Pinterest's page is ranking at the top organically.

If you have a board related to birthday party ideas, then there's a very high chance that people will see it through this link and visit your website or online store. It's a great way of driving traffic even if your site or online store is not ranking high in search engines. Finally, the biggest advantage of Pinterest is the lack of competition when compared to Facebook and Twitter. As very fewer marketers and companies are targeting Pinterest you as someone who has none or the least budget for marketing your business can use it for reaching more people and make handsome money online.

Suitable For

Almost anyone

Skills Required

- Ability to create Pins that are helpful, and actionable

- Ability to promote Pins on Pinterest Time Required To Get Started - Almost instant, if you are ready with your Pins just register on Pinterest and start pinning.

Tips

Set clear goals

Before you start pinning, first define your strategy. It means you need to know everything about your product, website, or service and how you are going to promote it on Pinterest.

Find the answers to the questions such as:

What niche are you going to operate?

What age group of audience is right for your niche?

Which are the authority Pinboards in your niche?

What kind of Pins is getting the highest Repins?

What are your favorite topics on which you can create Pins?

What are the best Pin designs?

Create your profile

Based on the research you've done in the first step, start creating your Pinterest profile. Here you'll need to enter your business name, profile picture, description about you, location, and website URL. Make sure you fill everything above by keeping your target audience in mind, and make it look relevant to them. Also, don't forget to add your website URL, when people visit your Pinterest profile they'll see the link to your site, and visit it. This is a great way of driving traffic so don't ignore this.

Post regularly

Posting new Pins regularly is a great practice. When you post regularly, there's a high chance that people will find your images in searches.
Also, your images appear in home feeds more often; this means that there's a great chance of users Repinning them and sharing them on their boards providing you more exposure.

Use relevant tags

Choosing the relevant hashtags is one of the most important factors when you need to give maximum exposure to your images. The right hashtags will bring your images in front of the right audience; this will help you to gather a responsive following who is interested in your niche. Before choosing your tags, think about the common terms that people might use to find your images, make a list of them, then use them as your hashtags.

Write detailed comments

When you upload or repin an image, Pinterest allows you to write a comment to describe the image. You should use this to tell people what the image is about. If you don't write anything, people won't get your message from the image. For example, take a look at the following image and its comment in the red box.

Add links

Another great feature of Pinterest is that it allows you to link your website, blog, online store, etc. to the image.

While uploading the image add the URL of your website or store, so when somebody clicks the image he will be redirected to your site or store.

Interact with your audience

Interacting with your audience is the key to finding success on Pinterest. Go and follow other boards in your niche and repin their posts. It will help you build relationships with other fellow users who will, in turn, reciprocate by following your boards.

How To Monetize

There are some good ways to make money from Pinterest; I am listing a few below. Go ahead with the way that suits you the most.

Sell your products

If you have a Shopify store where you sell your products, then you can sell them directly on Pinterest with Buyable Pins. To use Buyable Pins, you'll have to convert your account into a business account. Once you've upgraded to a business account, you can quickly implement Buyable Pins without any hassle

Website

If you already have a website in a particular niche, you can start creating content on products you want to promote along with your affiliate link. Now create a Pin related to the product and drive traffic from Pinterest your

Adsense Ads

If you don't want to promote any products you can post informative articles related to your niche on your blog, drive traffic from Pinterest and monetize by placing Adsense ads.

Chapter 3: Sell A Service On Fiverr

What is Fiverr.com?

A global online market called Fiverr offers tasks, services, and products for as little as $5.

Nearly 4.7 million people visit Fiverr each month.

Your goal should be to increase your customer base and increase sales by utilizing Fiverr's large visitor base.

On Fiverr, each service or task you offer is referred to as a GIG. You don't need to worry much about your gig's promotion or payment handling because Fiverr takes care of this for you thanks to its huge visitor base.

To maintain your ratings, all you need to do is concentrate on producing high-quality work because customer reviews will have a significant influence on whether or not your gig is successful.

On Fiverr, people provide a wide range of services, including anything you can imagine, including graphics and design, digital marketing, music and audio, and advertising.

Just keep in mind that $5 is just the minimum starting price; you can sell your gig for any amount.

Top Fiverr gig sellers utilize the platform and offer top-notch services to earn over $50,000 per year.

Suitable For

People who enjoy making other people's lives easier.

People who adore having the freedom to work at their ideal jobs.

Skills Necessary

- People with extensive knowledge in a particular field who can use that knowledge to make life easier for others by helping them complete tasks.

How Long Does It Take To Create A Gig On Fiverr?

On Fiverr, you can create a gig in less than an hour. Simply create an account on Fiverr first.
You must enter the title of your gig, upload an image for it, write a description for it, and add pertinent tags and keywords when creating a gig.

Tips

Find your strongest Skills

The first thing you must do is take a seat in silence, identify your strongest skills, and then stick to tasks involving those skills until you achieve some success.

For instance, if you can design logos and websites, you should create and market gigs on Fiverr that are centered on logo and website design.

Start by doing your homework.

To make sure that the gig you intend to offer has interested buyers, you must conduct some research before diving into the gig creation process.

What if your brilliant idea for a gig didn't pan out?

You must conduct the necessary research to comprehend what customers in your niche are looking for to avoid such a situation.

Look for lucrative jobs that fit your skill set.

Finding the well-liked gigs relevant to your skill set on Fiverr, studying them, and modeling your gig after them is one of the best ways to succeed.

The most crucial metrics you should consider while researching alternative jobs are:

- Title

- Description

- Image

- Pricing Methodology

- Upsell Technique

- Bonus Technique

Create a title for your gig.

Now that you have all the research data at your disposal, start creating gigs. Naturally, your first action will be to create a title.
The actions you must take to optimize the title of your gig are listed below.

Based on the results of your research, create a title for your gig using words that will catch the attention of and be relevant to your target audience.

For instance, say you are hiring someone to design a logo. You ought to think about utilizing headings like

I'll create three incredible logos in just 24 hours.

I'll create a PROFESSIONAL logo with no additional charge.

I'll create 2 BRILLIANT logos BONUS free editable document

All of the aforementioned titles are masterfully written because they contain two crucial elements.

First of all, they all contain intriguing words like BONUS, PROFESSIONAL, STUNNING, and MAGNIFICENT. These phrases undoubtedly aid in drawing in the appropriate audience.

Second, they all appeal to the key features that anyone looking to design a logo is considering.

For instance, the first title "3 MAGNIFICENT logos in 24 hours" will appeal to those who require a logo immediately.

People who want the option to include their changes in logo design will be drawn to the second title, "PROFESSIONAL logos with free revisions."

The third heading, "2 STUNNING logos BONUS Free editable file," will appeal to those who are familiar with logo design and wish to make their modifications.

Create a look for your gig.

You must have noticed when doing your initial research that some gigs have better images than others, which makes them stand out.

Make a short list of these pictures and use them as your inspiration when modeling your picture.

Use free online image editing tools like Pixlr or BeFunky to create the gig's image once you have the initial concept ready.

Write the gig's description

The description of your gig is crucial in persuading potential customers to place an order with you.

Therefore, you must make sure that the description of your gig is accurate, understandable, and compelling to potential customers.

To get some inspiration, look at the descriptions of other popular related gigs and base your own on them.

Never copy the description of another gig; doing so will result in your ban.

Simply draw inspiration from theirs when writing your description.

Additionally, to maintain the relevance of your gig, be sure to place it in the appropriate category.

Use right tags

The most crucial factor in helping your gig rank higher is tags.

The majority of people ignore them because they are unimportant, giving you the best chance to surpass them if you properly optimize your gig using precise tags.

In addition to the aforementioned considerations, you must ensure that your work on Fiverr is authentic and original.

There may be a lot of logo designers on Fiverr, but if you're the one who knows what your customers want and meets those needs, you'll be able to keep them as a client for a very long time.

How to Monetize

Money-making is very easy. The more orders you receive, the more money you make.

Your order placement is directly impacted by your delivery performance, which also affects user ratings.

The easy rule of thumb is that your orders will be more expensive as the higher the user ratings.

Fiverr secures every transaction you make, so you don't have to worry about any problems with payment processing.

If you have any reservations about this approach. Please use our contact form to get in touch with us.

Chapter 4 : Start Dropshipping Business

What is dropshipping?

Dropshipping is a term used in relation to online shopping. It's a technique where the online retailer doesn't manufacture or stock the item it sells.

Instead, the store first sells the item, then buys it at a discount from a different vendor and has it delivered right to the customer's address.

Dropshipping is a fantastic business model because it only requires setting up an online store, generating sales, and making money.

Stock, inventory, packing, shipping, or handling are not issues for you.

Because you don't have to buy a product until after you've made a sale and received payment from the customer, it's an excellent business model for someone with little money to invest.

In this business model, you essentially use customer money to buy a product and earn a profit without using your own money.

Appropriate For

Anyone who adores online shopping.

Skills Necessary

- Confident manner in dealing with customers and suppliers. You should be able to respond to their inquiries, resolve their issues, and impart sound advice.

- Strong verbal and written communication abilities.

- The capacity to recognize trends and opportunities and quickly adapt.

- Ability to analyze.

- Current expertise in the field.

Starting Points

The easiest way to get started is to create an account on Shopify.com.

Describe Shopify.com.

A website called Shopify gives you access to all the technical resources you'll ever need to set up your online store.

Nearly everything is available in one location, including hosting, domain names, designs, themes, and payment gateways.

With Shopify, setting up an online store is so simple that even people with little to no technical expertise can do it.

It's a fantastic option if you want to concentrate and spend more time on the activities that will help your business grow rather than on technical setup and maintenance.

Shopify is not just another website builder or content management system like WordPress. More than 70k people use it as a complete e-commerce platform to sell products online.

Tips

Choose your products to sell

Before you begin setting up your Shopify online store, make a list of the items you want to sell.

Anything is up for sale, including watches, t-shirts, necklaces, accessories, and more. Make a list of the things you like or are most interested in if you still can't decide what to sell; this will give you a direction

Perform preliminary research

After obtaining the list, you must do some investigating. Discover the responses to questions like:

Does the market have a need for the product you intend to sell?

What price range are people willing to accept?

Where do people go to purchase these goods?

Which social media platform has the best potential for attracting new customers?

What age range do your potential customers fall into?

What are the trends right now?

The best way to find the answers to the aforementioned questions is to visit reputable e-commerce sites like Amazon.com, identify the product designs that are selling the best, and read customer reviews to gain a deeper understanding of what customers are looking for.

To gather more information about your potential customers, you can also visit product forums, join social media groups, and visit well-known blogs.

This information will assist you in making the best product choices that will appeal to your target market and increase sales and profits for you.

For instance, if you want to sell wristwatches, go to Amazon.com and look at the best-selling models. Make a note of the price range, the designs, the customer reviews, and any other pertinent informatiom

Repeat the process above using other e-commerce websites that are comparable to Amazon. After that, continue to follow forums and fashion blogs to gather more information about your potential clients.

Locate the suppliers

Once you've decided on the goods you want to sell, you can look for the suppliers on websites like Everbuying.net or Alibaba.com.

Choose a few reputable suppliers, go over your marketing strategy with them, and determine whether they are a good fit for you and capable of delivering the products you have agreed upon on-time.

When you've finished the first three steps, it's time to set up your online store on Shopify.

Do this, sign up for an account on Shopify, validate your email, and then begin the store creation process.

You must select your unique domain name, theme, product category, and then add products here.

When adding products, you can use the Everbuying.net or Alibaba.com images and descriptions that your preferred supplier uses.

Pricing strategy

How much money you make will depend on your pricing strategy.
Determine the price of your product using the information you gathered during the research phase.

If you decide to sell wristwatches, for instance, and they cost you $17 each on Everbuying, and your research indicates that you should sell them for no more than $30, you can sell them for $27 and make $10 profit on each sale.

Promote your product links everywhere you want once you've added products to your Shopify store.

The best place to start your promotion campaign is on social media. To draw more customers to your store, you can also provide coupon codes.

Orders and shipping

As soon as someone places an order, use that money to order from your supplier on Everbuying or Alibaba, giving him the customer's shipping address.
Your supplier will personally arrange for shipping and packing. You have nothing to be concerned about.

The more targeted customers who come to your store and spend money, the more money you make.
If you have any reservations about this approach. Please use our contact form to get in touch with us.

Chapter 5: Write Articles On Authority Sites

Many reputable websites are constantly looking for new ideas and content to grow their user bases and increase profits.

They, therefore, require fresh talent who can carry out this task for them.

Even though the majority of them have teams dedicated to content research, curation, and editorial work, no matter how skilled they are, they are unable to cover all bases.

For this reason, a lot of these websites will pay you to write content for them. By doing this, they can identify fresh concepts and subjects that their content teams might not have come across otherwise.

It also gives writers a fantastic opportunity to make quick money writing articles without having to deal with the hassle of setting up and promoting their blogs.

Appropriate For

- People who enjoy writing and want to impart their knowledge and skills to others.

Skills Necessary

- The capacity to communicate ideas clearly and simply in writing.

Starting Points

Finding the subjects you are most interested in, doing some research, and writing an informative article is the best way to get started.

Then locate the authoritative websites in the related niche, get in touch with them via email, and send your article to them.

The Bonus List of 20 Amazing Authority Websites from a variety of niches is provided below; upon acceptance or publication, the majority of these websites will pay you up to $100 per article.

Finding a website that aligns with your interests and contributing as many educational articles there should be your goal.

Bonus List of 20 Amazing Authority Websites

1. Listverse.com

Topics Covered - General
Payment   - $100 per article
Payment Method - PayPal

2. Photoshop tutorials. ws

Topics Covered - Photoshop/Design
Payment   - $25 - $350 per article
Payment Method - PayPal

3. Blog.teamtreehouse.com

Topics Covered - Web Design
Payment   - $25 - $350 per article
Payment Method - PayPal

4. Thepennyhoarder.com

Topics Covered - Finance
Payment   - Up to $75 per article
Payment Method - PayPal

5. Ecommerceinsiders.com

Topics Covered - eCommerce
Payment   - $75 - $125 per article
Payment Method - Unspecified

6. Afineparent.com

Topics Covered - Parenting
Payment   - $100 per article
Payment Method - PayPal

7. Greatescapepublishing.com

Topics Covered - Travel
Payment   - $50 - $200 per article
Payment Method - Unspecified

8. Travelblog.viator.com

Topics Covered   - Travel
Payment   - $40 - $150 per article
Payment Method   - Unspecified

9. Uxbooth.com

Topics Covered - User Experience
Payment   - $100 per article
Payment Method   - Unspecified

10. Cracked.com

Topics Covered - General/Humor
Payment   - $50 - $200 per article
Payment Method   - PayPal

11. Code.tutsplus.com

Topics Covered - Web Development
Payment   - $100 - $250 per article
Payment Method   - Unspecified

12. Smashingmagazine.com

Topics Covered - Web Development/ UX
Payment   - $50 - $200 per article
Payment Method   - Unspecified

13. Alistapart.com

Topics Covered - Internet
Payment   - Up to $200 per article
Payment Method - Unspecified

14. Writenaked.net

Topics Covered   - Writing
Payment   - $50 - $200 per article
Payment Method - Unspecified

15. Metroparent.com

Topics Covered   - Parenting
Payment   - $35 - $350 per article
Payment Method   - Cheque

16. Internationalliving.com

Topics Covered - Living Overseas
Payment - $250 - $400 per article
Payment Method   - Unspecified

17. Sitepoint.com

Topics Covered - Web Development
Payment   - $150 - $200 per article
Payment Method - Unspecified

18. Digitalocean.com

Topics Covered   - Linux
Payment - $50 - $200 per article
Payment Method   - PayPal

19. Incomediary.com

Topics Covered - Make Money Online/SEO
Payment   - $50 - $200 per article
Payment Method - PayPal

20. Webloggerz.com

Topics Covered   - WordPress
Payment   - $30 - $100 per article
Payment Method   - Unspecified

Now that you have the list, start earning money by writing articles.

Chapter 6: Sell Quote Printables

What is a quote printable?

A quote printable is nothing more than a straightforward quote written in an artistic font on a beautifully designed canvas that can be printed.

Creatively created quote printables are very popular right now. Most people buy them, print their copies, put them in frames, and hang them on the walls of their homes and offices.

Placing inspirational quote printables on a wall enhances the aesthetics and helps people stay motivated all day.

You, as someone looking to earn money online, can take advantage of this chance to generate a steady income online.

I say this because there are many free online photo editing tools available today, which makes creating quote printables very simple.

You don't need to be an expert to use these tools; all you need is a little imagination and motivation to get going.

Appropriate For

- People with artistic and creative tendencies who enjoy imagining and designing.

Skills Necessary

- The ability to think creatively and to design and produce printables that can be sold online.

- The capacity to market your printables through blogging, guest posting, networking, and social media sites like Facebook, Instagram, and Twitter.

Designing Quote Printables Takes Time

The amount of time needed entirely depends on your background and design concepts. Using free online photo editing tools, you can start making printables right away once your design concept is complete.

Tips

Find some inspiration

It's best to find some inspiration and start coming up with ideas before you start thinking about the design of your quote printables.
In this case, visiting Pinterest.com is the best option for finding inspiration.

There is a sizable selection of gorgeously created printable quotes on Pinterest. Simply go to Pinterest and type in "quotes" or "quote printables," and you will be presented with a plethora of printables' images.

Start observing their layouts, typefaces, color schemes, and other elements now. This will undoubtedly inspire you to create a ton of printables.
The number of people who have pinned posts or images is another crucial statistic you should pay attention to.
More pins indicate that more people find the quote and its layout to be appealing.
Make a note of the image's layout and use it as a guide for your design, but never copy it.

For instance, look at the image below:

The fact that 3.2k people have pinned this quote printable, as shown in the red box, is a sure sign that people like it.

This can serve as inspiration for your designs.

Visit the following websites and type "quotes" or "quote printables" into the search bar to find even more ideas and inspiration:

- Onsuttonplace.com

- Printabledecor.net

Choose your tool in advance.

You need to use some tools to design printables, but there are so many options that it can be easy to become overwhelmed. I, therefore, advise choosing your tool in advance.

You can choose which tool is best for you from the list of tools I've provided below.

Start with one of the following free web tools if you want to get going right away without having to deal with installing any software:

- Picmonkey.com (fonts, themes, and overlays are excellent)

- Befunky.com

- Pixlr.com

- Fotor.com

- Use these software tools if you want more editing control:

- (Free) OpenOffice Impress (Powerpoint-like)

- (2010 version of Microsoft Powerpoint or later)

Amass all the necessary design materials.

You might need lovely images, fonts, icons, and vectors to make printable quotes of the highest caliber.

Below, I've listed a few websites that can help you get everything for free.

Images

- Pixabay.com

- Stocksnap.io

- Fonts:

- Fontsquirrel.com

- 1001fonts.com

- Icons:

- Flaticon.com

- Iconarchive.com

- Vectors

- Openclipart.org

Start - By this time, you should at least have a rough idea of your design, have chosen your tool, and have gathered all of your design materials. Create a printable version of a great quote right away.

How to Make Money

The following art-selling websites are the best places to sell your designs for the most money:

1.Fineartamerica.com

2.Cafepress.com

3.Imagekind.com

4.Redbubble.com

5.Society6.com

Numerous people go to the websites mentioned above in search of quote printables.

Each printable can be priced anywhere from $5 to $15.

When someone likes and purchases your printables, you will be paid. The more printables you sell, the more money you make.

Chapter 7: Become An Amazon Associate

What is the Amazon Associates Program?
With the help of the affiliate marketing program known as Amazon Associates, website owners, and bloggers can create links to Amazon and receive referral commissions whenever a website visitor clicks through and makes a purchase there.

Appropriate For

- People who enjoy writing, going into great detail, and wanting to impart their knowledge and skills to others.

- Best for individuals with a blog or website that already receives some daily traffic.

Skills Necessary

- The capacity to communicate ideas clearly and simply in writing.

- The capacity to persuade and convince others using the appropriate justification and argument.

How long does it take to become an Amazon Associate?

All you have to do is sign up on the Amazon website to become an affiliate. The name of your website must be entered when signing up.

If Amazon determines that your website complies with their standards and after reviewing it, they will accept you as an official Amazon associate.

It could take 2 to 5 days for the approval process.

Once you've been given the go-ahead, research the relevant products you want to promote on your blog, then copy and paste their affiliate links into your website.

Tips

Find products that are relevant to the content and readership of your website or blog.

This is the first and most crucial step.
The greater the product's relevance, the better your chances of making a sale.
For instance, it is extremely unlikely that you will make any sales by promoting watches on a blog that instructs readers how to perform yoga exercises.

However, you will have much more success if you try to promote yoga mats, pants, and books.

Include affiliate links in your content

The best way to get readers to click your affiliate links is to include plain text links within the body of an article.

More than any other part of a website, the page's main body of content is trusted by users.

Therefore, it is very likely that they will click the link if it is included in the body of the content.

Consider the following example: "Check out this cool [your aff link] smartwatch." It has maintained the top bestseller ranking for the past two months.

Connect product images to Amazon

Visuals are crucial for drawing in visitors.

Utilizing numerous, top-notch product images and turning them into clickable affiliate links is a quick and easy way to encourage people to click on your affiliate links.

One benefit of using Amazon is that you can freely use any product's image for marketing purposes on your website.

Write a product review article

Writing a great article and conducting a quality product review are two more effective ways to increase click-through rates and sales.

But before writing any reviews, make sure they are thorough and objective.

You shouldn't want people to believe that you are desperately trying to sell them the product.

A thorough review ought to address all queries and allay any doubts or concerns that any potential customer might have.
Ensure that your review addresses each of the points mentioned above.

Direct traffic to Amazon

One great aspect of Amazon is that it excels at converting site visitors into customers.
You don't need to follow them or advertise to them; Amazon will take care of everything else.
Simply directing them to Amazon.com using your affiliate link will do.

The great thing about this is that whenever someone uses your link to visit Amazon.com, you receive a portion of whatever they purchase for the following 24 hours (30 days after they added an item to their cart).

For instance, even if you didn't directly promote the wristwatch, you would still receive commissions if someone clicked on your "Yoga Mat" affiliate link, visited Amazon.com, and purchased two wristwatches instead of a yoga mat within 24 hours.

Develop reader loyalty and trust

Your readers' loyalty and trust in you and your website will significantly increase your sales.
The majority of your sales will come from regular, devoted readers.
Readers who consistently connect with you and learn to trust you and your website after some time.

As a result, they are more likely to follow your recommendations or reviews than those of someone they don't trust.

How to Make Money

The monetization formula resembles the majority of the other techniques covered in this app almost exactly.

You earn more money when more people use your affiliate link to visit Amazon.com and make purchases.

You don't need to worry about it because Amazon.com will take care of all the payment and commission processing for you.

Chapter 8: Resell Items On eBay

What is eBay.com?

The most popular online marketplace for buying and selling goods is eBay.

It is a location where individuals and companies can buy or sell new or used goods, including almost anything from books and clothes to cars.

Here is how eBay functions:

Almost anything, from antiques to mobile phones, books to sporting goods, is listed on eBay by a seller.

The seller decides whether to set a fixed price for the item or only accept bids (auction-style listing).

When a listing is set up as an auction, bidding starts at a price the seller specifies and lasts on eBay for a predetermined number of days.

The item is then put up for bid by buyers. The bidder with the highest offer wins when the listing expires.

In a fixed-price listing, the item is awarded to the first buyer who offers to pay the seller's asking price.

Appropriate For

- Self-motivated people who know how to use online and offline platforms to spread the word to their friends, family, acquaintances, and total strangers.
-

Skills Necessary

- Along with a business-savvy mind, some prior experience with selling products offline or online is welcome.

How Long Does It Take To Start Selling On eBay?

You first need an eBay account and a PayPal account to start selling.

The next step is to register your product, for which you must upload some images and create a compelling description.

Even a novice can complete all the aforementioned tasks in one or two days.

Tips

Obtaining some feedback before beginning to sell anything is a good practice if you are brand-new to eBay and your account has no feedback.

Nowadays, people are very cautious when making purchases online, so if your account has no feedback, no one will buy anything from you.

It is advised that you obtain at least 10 to 15 reviews before selling anything.

Purchase 10–15 items for $0.99 with free shipping for the quickest and easiest way to get feedback.

Many sellers give you positive feedback right away after receiving payment.

Start small

The majority of eBay resellers purchase a large quantity of a given product at a wholesale price before selling it on eBay for a retail price.

If you don't have the funds to purchase wholesale stock, make a list of all the good-condition unwanted items you currently have in your home.

Research

Now that you have a short list of items that are prepared for sale, you need to make sure there is a market for them.

Spend ten minutes Googling your item to find out what it's worth on eBay and a few other e-commerce sites.

Because you'll be aware of your product's market and pricing strategies, you'll be able to sell the right products more aggressively.

Additionally, find relevant, targeted keywords that will make it easier for people to find your products on Google.

Crafting the title is the single most crucial step in capturing the interest of a potential customer.

Make sure your title is catchy, comprehensive, and contains the right keywords.

For this, you don't need to be a tech whiz. Simply consider what a potential purchaser of this item would enter in the search bar.

Write the item's description

 Complete all the fields in your listing and ensure that your textual description contains all the details that a potential buyer might be interested in.

The majority of the lazy sellers ignore this and have terrible success on eBay.

Upload the item's images

Only include high-quality images. Make sure the product is depicted in fresh, clear (not blurry), and comprehensive photographs.

Additionally, upload at least 6 pictures rather than just 2 or 3.

- Timing

Most experienced sellers start their 10-day listings on Thursday. You should do the same because it will give you two weekends' worth of exposure. Weekends are usually when you see the most traffic.

How to Make Money

Money-making is very easy.

The more orders you receive, the more money you make.
User feedback is influenced by the item's quality and delivery, which has an immediate impact on your order placement.
Therefore, be certain that the goods you deliver are of high quality.

You don't have to be concerned about any payment processing issues because eBay handles all of your transactions securely.

When you reach the point of making a profit, buy a lot of your best-selling items at a discount and then sell them for retail to boost your profits.

Chapter 9: Become Social Media Evaluator

Social media is now a significant aspect of everyone's lives.

If I'm not mistaken, you probably check your various social media accounts for at least 20 to 30 minutes each day.

If so, why not make use of this time to earn money online?

Nowadays, the majority of businesses and brands run social media campaigns to increase user engagement, market products, and keep up an online presence.

They, therefore, employ social media analysts to carry out these tasks more effectively.

Regular social media users like you are evaluators because they assist large corporations in managing their accounts, tracking the success of their campaigns, and learning what works and what doesn't.

The demand for these types of jobs has significantly increased in recent years. You can benefit from this chance and use social media to earn money as well.

Appropriate For

- Anyone who enjoys social media and uses it frequently.

Skills Necessary

- The capability to work independently, analyze results, and adhere to project deadlines.

- The capacity to communicate ideas and emotions in English clearly both orally and in writing.

Things You'll Need

- An individual Facebook, Twitter, Instagram, or Pinterest account.

- Consistent usage of all social media platforms.

Starting Points

Applying to be a Social Media Evaluator on Appen.com is the best way to get started.

What is Appen.com.

To make their social media campaigns more relevant to their target audience, Appen helps web-based businesses and brands.

Your responsibility as a social media evaluator will be to assess the newsfeed of various social media platforms and offer suggestions.

You might need to work on Instagram, Facebook, Twitter, etc., depending on the project you've been given.

You must fill out an application with your personal information, education, work experience, qualifications, and resume to join Appen.

The Appen team will then review your application to see if you are qualified for the position.
Once accepted, you'll have a week to finish a qualification process for which the Appen team will provide all the necessary instructions and materials.

When the qualification process is complete, projects will be assigned to you right away. You must finish the assigned tasks to receive payment.

A different website

You can also sign up at the website below, which also offers similar social media jobs to Appen if you want to increase your income as a social media evaluator.

Be-a-virtual-assistant.timeetc.com

Expected Income

At Appen.com, you can typically expect to make $13.75 per hour as an independent social media assessor. Payment occasionally varies according to the position and the nation in which you live.

Depending on the availability of work, you can work anywhere between 12 and 30 hours per week. When any work becomes available, the Appen team will send you an email.

Make sure you have a functioning bank account in your name because Appen only pays via bank transfer (wire transfer).

Chapter 10:Start A Blog

One of the simplest ways to make money from home is as a blogger.

If you are blogging from home, it differs from any other job. You don't have to work from 9 to 5.

You can easily work at any time of the day.

But be aware that it may take some time for blogging to generate income for you.

So I advise you to enter this field gradually.

Don't quit your day job if you have one. Start your blog part-time.

It's best to switch to full-time blogging mode once it reaches the point where it is earning you more than your comfortable thresholds.

Appropriate For

- People who enjoy writing and want to impart their knowledge and skills to others.

Skills Necessary

- The capacity to communicate ideas clearly and simply in writing.

How Long Does It Take To Start A Blog?

Your level of expertise will determine how long it takes; if you are an expert, you can easily start a blog within a few hours.
A day or two would be enough for a total beginner to have the fundamental setup ready.

Tips

Create a blog about a subject in which you excel.

Start a travel blog, for instance, if you enjoy traveling and have been to many locations.

Constantly try to confine your blog to a single domain.

Avoid including content from several domains in one blog.
Writing about cooking advice on a fashion blog, for instance.
Keep your blog limited to a single domain.

- Try to produce incredibly exceptional and one-of-a-kind content using your experience and knowledge.

- Try to provide your readers with a lot of value.

- Write about a subject that will affect your readers' lives.

- Pay attention to your blog's audience.

Try to find solutions to the issues they are having. Continually respond to their comments. alleviate their discomfort.

- Stick with your blog. A blog is similar to a marriage.

It will thrive if you show it some affection. It will die if you ignore it.

Being half-hearted in your blogging efforts is pointless because if you don't care, why should anyone else?

- Consider the audience, style, tone of voice, and content.

Take a look at those who are already executing your plan. Consider the following inquiries for yourself:

How can I distinguish myself from the crowd?

What more can I add that hasn't been said?

What sets me apart from other people?

What motivates me to do this?

- Maintain a professional demeanor as you manage and expand your blog.

- .Never criticize other businesses, bloggers, or individuals. Keep in mind that everything is connected.

You don't want what you've said to come back to haunt you in the future.

- Be flexible and eager to work with other creatives

You'll get to know some amazing and inspiring people

How to Make Money

By writing an informative article or posting banner ads on your blog's pertinent pages, you can monetize your blog by endorsing goods or services associated with its subject. When someone purchases a product you've recommended, you may receive sizable commissions.

You can also use Google Adsense to monetize your blog. Your revenue will increase as more people click on your ad.

Chapter 11: Publish A Kindle eBook

Another easy method of producing passive income consistently is to publish a Kindle eBook.

Did you know that, compared to other search engines like Yahoo or Bing, Amazon.com is Google's biggest rival?

Amazon sees more product searches than any other conventional search engine combined.

People look for highly regarded books on Amazon rather than blog posts on Google when they want in-depth information on a particular subject.

Your goal should be to take advantage of Amazon.com's expanding influence and popularity in order to establish a reliable passive income source.

Appropriate For

- People who are well-versed in a particular subject or who enjoy conducting research and disseminating their findings.

Skills Necessary

- The capacity to offer in-depth analysis on a specific subject.

- The capacity to offer some extraordinary advice for resolving issues faced by others.

How Long Does It Take to Create an eBook?

The amount of time needed is entirely up to the author of the eBook. What subjects does he/she wish to cover? How much information does the author want to provide?

These are the key elements that determine the amount of time needed.

Tips

Conduct thorough research.

A Kindle eBook product needs to succeed.
Investigate what people are looking for in the area that is related to the subject of your eBook.
Look at how many people are searching for yoga exercises to lose weight on the internet and Amazon, for instance, if you are writing an eBook on the topic. What do they hope to get out of a book?
Studying the comments, reviews, and popularity of the competitor's books that are already available on Amazon will make it simple for you to conduct this research.

Create content with just one reader in mind.

You can tell how much a reader already knows when you are familiar with them.
By giving him/her only the information they need, you can avoid boring them with obvious information.

Use search engines like **Yahoo** Answers, **WikiAnswers**, **Quora**, and others to see how many people are asking questions about the subject you've chosen.

More inquiries indicate a greater demand for solutions, which is encouraging.

Keep an eye out for market gaps in your chosen domain.

Additionally, check to see if there is a demand for a particular subject and if your eBook can meet that need.
Check Amazon.com to see how many books are available in the area you chose. Do people still purchase those books?

You will gain a better understanding of the market's demand and purchasing power as a result.

Identify a few amiable readers who fit your ideal reader profile and present them with your first draft.

They will not only improve your book, but they will also make you feel more self-assured.

How to Make Money

Enroll in the Kindle Direct Publishing Program, which grants Amazon the sole right to distribute your Kindle eBook.

This will enable you to market your eBook widely at launch by allowing you to sell it in every country where Amazon.com is accessible.

Make a small niche website about the associated subject and advertise your eBook there. You earn more money the more eBooks you sell.

Chapter 12: Start A YouTube Channel

The simplest way to make money online is to launch a Youtube channel, which requires no money upfront.

The fact that YouTube receives almost 5 billion daily video views attests to its dominance online.

The owner of the PewDiePie YouTube account, Felix Kjellberg, made $12,000,000 in 2015 from just one YouTube channel.

If you take advantage of the current opportunity that YouTube offers, you too could experience success.

Appropriate For

- Those who enjoy making videos, speaking in front of cameras, or making documentaries or short films.

Skills Required

- The capacity to record videos with a camcorder or mobile device or to create videos using software tools.

How long does it take to launch a YouTube channel?

You can start almost immediately. You must create a channel on YouTube.com and upload videos there.

Tips

- Establish a YouTube channel with a focus on a particular subject, such as humor, tutorials, recipes, etc. Don't just start a channel for random, unrelated videos.

For instance, if you enjoy gadgets, you can start a gadget reviews channel where you can post videos reviewing the newest gadgets and assist viewers in making the best decision possible.
Choose a subject that truly interests you.

- Examine other videos that are related to your topic and look at the number of views they receive.

You can use it to get a general sense of how popular your subject is.
In general, the theme is more advantageous the more views it receives given that more people are looking for it.

- Examine the current videos related to your theme to see if there is any information that is missing.

To increase the number of views on your videos, you can cover these topics.

- Use all of your effort to interact with your audience. Analyze the feedback that viewers leave on your videos to discover the underlying expectations that they have of you.

- Try to learn what they enjoy and dislike about your videos

Find out why certain videos have the highest retention rates by studying them.

6.Monitor your rivals and try to imitate the strategies that are successful for them. However, never attempt to imitate them; always maintain your originality.

- Always make an effort to improve on the previous video in each new one.

Therefore, you ought to reflect on how terrible I was in my early videos when you watch them again after a while.

That's encouraging because it demonstrates your growth.

- Repeat the experimentation process

Never be afraid to experiment and see what works.

The only way to discover novel and exciting ideas that will put you miles ahead of your rivals is through experiments.

- Lastly, try collaborating with other YouTubers who are creating content that is similar to yours.

Discover their methods and outlook. For your channel, teamwork can work wonders. Enjoy yourself. Enjoy life by doing the things you love.

How to Make Money

The general YouTube monetization rule is very straightforward. You'll make more money if your videos receive more views. Simply enable the monetize option in your YouTube channel settings to get started.

It is very easy.

Chapter 13: Sell PLR

What is a PLR?

Private Label Rights, or PLR, is the abbreviation. It's a license that any product creator offers, and if you buy it, you get complete freedom to do whatever you want with the thing you just bought.

With a PLR license in your possession, you can brand the purchased product as your own, credit you as the author, change the words and graphics, divide it into several parts, and more.

In short, you can use the product however you like.

Most importantly, PLR enables you to set your price for the product when you resell it. Because you only need to invest once to purchase the product and its PLR license, it offers excellent return on investment.

Then, you can sell the item as many times as you like and keep all of the profits without having to give a portion to the product's original creator.

For illustration, suppose you spent $50 to purchase an eBook and the PLR license for it. If you sold 200 copies of that eBook for $70 each, your total profit would be $1350 ($1400 - $50).

PLR offers a fantastic opportunity for someone who wants to earn money quickly without having to put in the time necessary to create a quality product.

Where can I purchase goods with PLR licenses?

You can purchase PLR goods from a variety of online markets. I've listed a few reputable websites below:

- Theplrstore.com

- Idplr.com

- Bigcontentsearch.com

- Master-resale-rights.com

- Plr. me

- Plrassassin.com

- Surefirewealth.com

How to Make Money

Provide paid membership courses

Divide your product into several comprehensible components and place each one in an autoresponder.
Offer a paid membership with a monthly fee of $15 to $30.

Your autoresponder will automatically send them to your subscribers on a weekly or monthly basis when someone joins your membership.

Develop your own product

You can combine several PLRs to develop a unique product on your own. Selling your product has the potential to bring in sizable profits.

Create an email list by providing any PLR eBook or report to your visitors as a lead magnet in exchange for their email.
You can then promote affiliate offers to your subscribers and earn significant commissions once you have a sizable email list.

Start a blog

You can break up PLR products into different parts and use those parts to create articles. These articles can help you expand your blog and monetize it by running ads and promoting affiliate products.

Chapter 14: Start Data Entry Work

Today, data entry is one of the most sought-after online jobs. If you have looked online for ways to make money, I'm confident you have read about it before.

Reading data from one source and entering it into another is a typical data entry task.

Data entry tasks include, for instance, reading information from a PDF report and typing it into an Excel spreadsheet.

These days, a lot of businesses gather a ton of information about their customers, their products, their research, and so forth.

They gather these data using a variety of channels, including their website, social media, forums, surveys, and so forth.

They must combine all of this data, which has been gathered from various sources, onto one platform so that they can study and analyze it.

Businesses need individuals who can perform this data entry work for them to accomplish this.

Most businesses hire independent home-based contractors to perform data entry work for them as part of an outsourcing arrangement with another company.

You now have a fantastic opportunity to make money online.

Appropriate For

- most people.

Skills Necessary

- Quick and accurate typing abilities.

- Basic computer knowledge

- Proven proficiency with word processors like Microsoft Word.

- A reliable computer with an internet connection that is fast.

Starting Points

Despite the fact that data entry jobs are very popular, it has become very challenging to locate reliable data entry firms because of the numerous data entry scams that are active online.

You should exercise extreme caution before enrolling in any alleged data entry program, is my advice to you.

Also keep in mind that reputable businesses will never demand payment for you to apply for one of their data entry jobs.

I've listed three trustworthy websites/URLs where you can apply to work as a data entry clerk to give you a head start.

- Tdec.com

(Exact URL - http://www.tdec.com/contact-us/job-opportunities)

- Diondatasolutions.net

(Exact URL - http://www.diondatasolutions.net/opportunities.htm)

- Axiondata.com

(Exact URL - http://axiondata.com/employment.htm)

Expected Earnings

Traditionally, working from home data entry jobs won't pay much because the work is irregularly available.

Earnings are inconsistent because you might find work one day but not the next.
Although data entry won't make you wealthy, it's a good way to make use of your downtime and make some extra cash.

Chapter 15:Sell A Video Course On Udemy

What is Udemy.com?

An online learning marketplace is called Udemy.

It offers a vast selection of classes in subjects like yoga, photography, programming, and much more.

A course can be made in text, audio, or video formats. Every course is available on demand, allowing students to study whenever, wherever, and on any device they choose.

Appropriate For

- people who enjoy problem-solving, teaching, and explanation.

Skills Necessary

- Extensive expertise in any field of your choice.

- The capacity to communicate knowledge understandably.

- The capacity to produce and record excellent videos.

How Long Does It Take To Create A Video Course?

Depending on the course's length, the number of modules it contains, and the amount of preparation time needed.

Tips

- Decide on a subject in which you have expertise

- Research the courses that are pertinent to your subject and find out how many students have signed up for them.

This will give you a general idea of the people who are curious about your subject and prepared to pay for your course.

- Research the competing courses to see what you can add that will set your course apart from them and make it significantly better.

- After determining your audience's skill level, develop the course material.

For instance, you must first choose whether your course is intended for beginners or experts.

Consequently, you must design your course material so that it appeals to the appropriate audience.

- Ensure that your course's title and description are written to attract the attention of your intended audience.

In your course description, make an effort to respond to the frequently asked questions from your audience.
Use the video for at least 80% of your course because it is the most interactive format.
Additionally, try to keep each video lesson's length between 2 and 10 minutes.

- Establish a connection with the crowd and engage them.

For an engaging and interactive experience, you can always conduct quizzes in between lectures.

How to Make Money

Since Udemy receives a lot of daily traffic, there is a good chance that people will find your course, enroll in it, and you will begin to make money.

You could even start a small blog to promote your course and discuss topics related to it. The more students who enroll in your course, the more money you make.

Chapter 16: Become A Graphic Designer

Because graphics grab our attention and draw us to products and brands, graphic design is among the most crucial elements for businesses.

Consider your reaction if your recently purchased iPhone arrived in a box that was shoddy in design and dull in color. Unhappy, I presume?

In the eyes of the customer, quality graphics help to build the brand's reputation and leave a lasting good impression.

The proliferation of new businesses brought on by the development of the internet and technology has made the need for eye-catching graphics essential to many industries.

This explains why there is a constant need for graphic designers.

Anyone who wants to earn money online can take advantage of this chance to improve their situation.

The majority of your work as a graphics designer will involve creating websites, logos, print headers, illustrations, and product interfaces.

Appropriate For

- Designers, painters, and artists.

Skills Necessary

- Imagination and creativity.

- Knowledge of current fashions and trends.

- The capacity to invent and produce designs.

- The ability to use programs like Photoshop to convert designs into digital format.

- Ability to manage your time, meet deadlines and work within budget.

How To Get Started

You can find graphic design jobs by visiting the following websites/URLs:

- 99designs.com

(Exact URL - https://99designs.com/designers)

- Graphicriver.net

(Exact URL - https://graphicriver.net/become-an-author)

- Coroflot.com

(Exact URL - http://www.coroflot.com/apply-now)

- Dribble.com

(Exact URL - https://dribbble.com/jobs?location=Anywh ere)

- Behance.net

(Exact URL - https://www.behance.net/joblist)

- Designweek.co.uk

(Exact URL - https://jobs.designweek.co.uk/jobs/graphic s)

- Designjobsboard.com

Expected Earnings

You can anticipate making between $15 and $35 per hour as a beginning graphics designer. At the intermediate level, you can anticipate making $35 to $60 per hour.

Once you have a lot of experience and good reviews, you can expect to earn $65 to $100 or more per hour.

Chapter 17:Be A Proofreader

What is Proofreading?

Simply put, proofreading involves carefully reading any text to identify and fix grammatical, spelling, and style errors.

The need for high-quality content is increasing steadily as a result of the growth of the internet, blogs, and social media.

Because of this, there is a high demand for online proofreaders who can check any text for errors.

You should take advantage of this chance to make good money online.

Appropriate For

- Anyone who enjoys reading, writing, and finding and fixing mistakes.

Skills Necessary

- The ability to write and speak English fluently, like a native.

- The capacity to work independently and with excellent comprehension of written material.

- A word-per-hour proofreading rate of 1000–1500.

Starting Points

Applying for a position as an online proofreader on the following two websites is the best way to get started:

- The website ProofreadingServices.com

Fill out an application for ProofreadingServices at

http://www.proofreadingservices.com/page
s/careers

You must pass a 20-question test that lasts
20 minutes to submit your application. Your
proficiency with English and grammar
basics will be tested by these questions.

To increase your chances of being accepted,
try to get as many questions as possible
correct.

Your chances of being chosen are increased
the higher your test score.

- Scribendi.com 2.

Fill out an application on Scribendi at
https://www.scribendi.com/employment.en
.html#telecommute

With Scribendi, proofreaders have a lot of freedom in terms of when and which projects they work on.

But you must promise to proofread at least 10,000 words each month.
comparable to ProofreadingServices.com Although Scribendi doesn't hold eligibility screenings, applicants with experience in editing, writing, document creation, or language teaching have a higher chance of being hired.

PayPal is used to send payments, and there are monthly bonuses available.

Chapter 18: Do Affiliate Marketing

Affiliate marketing: What is it?
When a customer purchases a product after being referred by an affiliate's own marketing efforts, the business pays the affiliate a certain percentage of commission. This is known as affiliate marketing.

Appropriate For

- People who enjoy communicating verbally and in writing, and who can persuade others.

Skills Necessary

- Being able to advertise products online using social media, videos, and other methods.

Starting an affiliate marketing campaign takes time almost immediately. Selecting an online product that pays you a commission when you advertise and sell it using your affiliate link is all that is required.

Tips

- Choose an online product from the industry that you are knowledgeable about. Choose a product related to diet, for instance, if you are a dietician.

Every domain has a wide range of products; all you have to do is choose one that fits your needs.

- Product-finding websites include Clickbank.com, Shareasale.com, and Jvzoo.com. Thousands of products from numerous domains are listed on these websites.

- Pick a product that pays you a commission of at least 50% on each sale.

- You don't need to worry about how you'll get your commissions because the majority of product websites handle affiliate link creation and payouts.

Simply ask the vendor to create your unique affiliate link, then start promoting it.

- Promote your affiliate link on social networks like Facebook, Twitter, Digg, StumbleUpon, and Reddit if you want to make money right away from affiliate marketing.

How to Make Money

Simply encourage more people to purchase the product using your affiliate link to start earning money.

Make a Facebook page or banner ads to advertise the product.
Describe how the product will assist customers in resolving their issues.
Increase people's understanding of the subject and assist them in resolving other related issues.

Chapter 19: Become An Online Tutor

The convenience of online coaching is preferred by many people these days due to the rise in busy lifestyles.

The experience of online coaching is now incredibly realistic thanks to the development of technology and the internet. As a result, there is a rapid increase in demand for online tutors. So, if you enjoy assisting others in their learning, online tutoring might be your ticket to financial success.

Appropriate For

- people with a passion for instructing others and a gift for knowledge transfer.

Skills Necessary

- Possess expertise in any field you wish to teach, including math, science, computer programming, etc.

- two years of completed study in the subject you wish to teach or a college degree.

- Online tutoring experience is a plus, but it's not required.

Starting Points

- The first and best option is to sign up with an online tutoring service, which will assign you, students, by your schedule and profile.

The list of reputable websites for online tutoring is as follows:

1.Tutor.com

2.TutorVista.com

3.e-Tutor.com

4.SmarThinking.com

5.Starting on your own is the second option.

Create a local flier or advertisement with your credentials and contact details, then post it on community bulletin boards, in grocery stores, and libraries.
Ask them to tell their family and friends.
Create a Facebook page for your virtual tutoring program and ask your online contacts to like and share it.

Expected Income

Depending on your reputation and experience, you can expect to make between $9 and $40 per hour.

You can charge more than $50 per hour if you hold a teaching credential and are an expert in subjects like advanced math, science, statistics, and computer programming.

Chapter 20: Become A Ghostwriter

Exactly who writes ghosts?

A ghostwriter is simply someone who writes on behalf of other people.
The majority of busy bloggers, authors, and publishers employ ghostwriters to finish their writing projects.
The client who hires you as a ghostwriter will own the finished product.

You will never be credited as an author anywhere. However, you'll be paid well for the work.
Writing books, eBooks, blog posts, articles, and press releases will make up the majority of your writing assignments as a ghostwriter.

Appropriate For

- Those who are passionate about writing.

Skills Necessary

- The capacity to comprehend the needs of clients and translate their stories into writing.

Starting Points

You can begin by going to the following websites and submitting an application for the available ghostwriting jobs there:

- Upwork.com

- Freelancer.com

- WriteZillas.com

(Exact URL - http://writezillas.com/freelance-ghostwrite rs.html)

- Jobforwriter.com

(Exact URL - http://jobforwriter.com/ghostwriting.php)

- Peopleperhour.com

(Exact URL https://www.peopleperhour.com/freelance-ghostwriting-jobs)

Expected Earnings

You can anticipate making $10 to $25 per hour as an entry-level employee. At the intermediate level, you can anticipate making $30 to $50 per hour.

Once you have a lot of experience and good reviews, you can expect to earn $60 to $70 per hour.

Chapter 21: Start Copywriting

What is copywriting, exactly?

Copywriting is the process of creating written material for marketing or advertising. The aim of the copy is to influence someone's thinking or persuade them to buy a product.

Suitable For

- Those who are enthusiastic writers.

Skills Required

- The capacity to write copy that will persuade readers and boost product sales.

How long does it take to get a copy started?

It will take some time for you to learn the psychological underpinnings and principles of writing effective copy, depending on how quickly you pick things up.

How to Get Rich

- Successful copywriters receive handsome compensation for each piece of copy they produce. At first, you might not make much money, but as you become more skilled, no one can stop you from earning hundreds of thousands of dollars by publishing just a few hundred copies.

- You might begin by crafting a pitch for the product you're endorsing. Analyze the results and try your best to get better.

- As a freelance copywriter, you can earn money by marketing your services.

Easily register on the following websites to become a copywriter:

1.Iwriter.com

2.Textbroker.com

3.Writer access.com

4.Upwork.com

Chapter 22:Do Email Marketing

What is it?

Another type of affiliate marketing is email marketing, in which you use your blog's email list of subscribers to advertise a specific product.

Appropriate For

- People who enjoy communicating verbally and in writing, and who can persuade others.

Skills Necessary

- Ability to write email marketing copy.

- Building an email list takes time.

Although it takes time to build an email list, email marketing is very profitable.

You will offer a free ebook or email course—anything that will be of use to them—in exchange for their email address to build an email list.

In exchange for their email addresses, blog readers who already read your blog can sign up for your weekly newsletter by filling out an opt-in form.

Building an email list that is profitable in size typically takes between one and three months.

However, in the long run, an email list is one of the most lucrative and reliable sources of passive income.

How to Make Money

- Email your email list with promotional materials that include affiliate links to the products you are promoting.

The likelihood that more people will click on your affiliate links and buy the product increases the larger your email list.

Consequently, by receiving affiliate commissions, you make more money.

Chapter 23: Start A Book Review Site

Describe a book review website.
A book review website is, as the name implies, a website where reviews of books are published.

Appropriate For

- people who are passionate about reading.

Skills Necessary

- Ability to write a thorough, frank, and versatile book review.

How Long Does It Take To Launch A Book Review Website?

A website can practically be launched in a few hours. In this instance, building a website is not a difficult task; however, giving frank and interesting reviews is.

Giving reviews for a respectable number of books won't be difficult if you've read a lot of books since you were a child.

However, I won't advise you to go this route if you're just starting to read books because it might take a while to read a sizable number of books and then write reviews.

How to Make Money

- Become a partner with Amazon. Use the Amazon affiliate links on your website to promote books.

- Encourage people to purchase books using your affiliate links by using your reviews.

You'll make more money if more people use your affiliate link to purchase books.

Chapter 24:Start Your Podcast

A podcast is what?

A series of digital audio files that can be downloaded to a computer or portable media player from the Internet. Subscribers can receive new installments of these files automatically.

Appropriate For

- Individuals who enjoy explaining things and talking.

Skills Necessary

- Extensive knowledge of any subject you find interesting.

- The capacity for logical argumentation.

The amount of time needed to create a podcast
A podcast is made in three crucial steps.
Create a script, first. Identify the topic for the content. To remember what you are going to talk about or promote, outline.

- Take voiceovers for your podcast.

- Place your podcast on your individual iTunes website.

How to Make Money

1.Sell your podcast first. However, make sure the podcast's content is interesting to persuade listeners to pay for it.

2 .Make money by including a commercial in your podcast.

Chapter 25: Facebook Marketing

What is Facebook marketing?

Facebook marketing, which involves advertisers promoting products on Facebook, is an additional form of affiliate marketing.

Suitable For

- People who use Facebook for fun.

Skills Required

- The ability to create Facebook posts and images that are aesthetically pleasing.

- The option of Facebook page promotion.

- The ability to persuade others with sound reasoning.

It takes time to launch a Facebook marketing campaign.

You can start using Facebook marketing right away by making promotional posts and a page to promote a product.
This can be finished in a short amount of time.

How to Get Rich

- Boost the number of people who visit your Facebook page.

- Start promoting any affiliate products associated with the Facebook page's theme.

- If at all possible, use Facebook ads to spread the word about your posts and pages to a larger audience.

- You will make more money if more people use your affiliate link to buy more products.

CONCLUSION

In conclusion, "THE ULTIMATE REMOTE JOBS GUIDEBOOK"provides a comprehensive guide for individuals seeking flexible and remote employment opportunities. It highlights the benefits of remote work, offers practical advice on finding legitimate online jobs, and emphasizes the importance of time management and self-discipline. As the world continues to evolve, this book serves as a valuable resource for anyone looking to harness the power of the digital age and create a fulfilling career from the comfort of their own home. Embrace the possibilities, stay motivated, and embark on a journey toward a successful and balanced work-from-home experience.

www.ingramcontent.com/pod-product-compliance
Lightning Source LLC
Chambersburg PA
CBHW072205290526
45794CB00004B/1657